# THE MISERY OF THE GOOD CHILD

J.D. GILL. PHD

Create Space
2015

BOOKS BY J.D. GILL


FORMS OF LIFE and other essays
LETTERS TO JIM
FINDING HUMAN
LETTERS OF JULIET to the Knight in Rusty Armor
100 REASONS WHY I LOVE YOU

Be self-indulgent, and those who are also self-indulgent will like you. Tear your neighbor to pieces, and the other neighbors will laugh. But if you beat your soul, all souls will cry out.


--Jean-Paul Sartre

# CONTENTS

# THE GOOD CHILD

All persons have limits. Consequently, all parents have limits. It is routine for us to discipline or punish our children when they exceed our limits. Unconsciously our goal in doing this is to get them to behave in ways we can more easily tolerate and manage. Besides it makes our load lighter. It is routine in these interactions for us to feel we are helping the child by our actions. They can't just go around upsetting people. The world, after all, has limits, and the child needs to learn about these.

This is a way of saying parents have different bandwidths of what they can and cannot handle. Some parents are extremely rigid and can only manage little breadth. Some, on the other hand, can manage a wide range with seeming ease.

From the child's perspective, however, the picture may not be so clear.

First of all the child picks up a mixed message. The over the table message is "this is for your own good." The under the table message is "this is my limit; I can't go any farther." That is the parent is being incapable. What now? The child is likely to be puzzled if not frightened.

In such situations the child routinely finds, through repeated interactions, what behaviors on his or her part result in upset from the parents and which do not. Avoiding negative consequences is clearly an important task in childhood (unless the context is too chaotic or impossible). This allows for a solution. The child is able to think: I know how to manage this situation. I will limit my actions and interactions to this bandwidth where the parent seems to be okay, and then I will avoid eighty percent of parental negatives. What a clever child I am! These people are easy, &c.

Such a discovery on the child's part allows for easier sailing around the house.

But what has happened? The child has essentially put on what might be called a "behavioral corset." That is the child has hidden parts of him or herself and only allowed certain (approved) parts to be seen. The child has *limited* his or her bandwidth to match the bandwidth of the parent. As long as the child is able to stick to this strategy, the pond will stay tolerably smooth.

Winnicott (1992) described this process as the development of a "false self." His idea was that in such a context the false self is more acceptable than the real self. My parents *like* that one. They say things like, "Pam is really growing up." What is left over from this false self, the real self, is saved for times when the parents are away.

If my parents are abusive and hurt me when they reach their limits (i.e. don't like what I am doing or saying), I will be terrified, and I won't know what to do. I may develop hyper-acuity and scan them for any sign of displeasure before I even think of doing anything. I may simply freak out and be crippled by fear.

The child who limits his or her behavior to avoid negative consequences will typically feel he or she has mastered the system and has improved his or her lot because it is now possible to avoid a good deal of negativity. The parents also will be pleased.

*Psychologically, however, the child is not taking care of him or herself as much as he or she is taking care of the parents*

The child is behaving and speaking in the way he or she is, because it does not upset the parent. Thus the parent needs this behavior on the part of the child in order for the parent to maintain coping ability.

*The child learns the way to be okay in the world is to take care of others.*

That is the child learns his or her well being depends on what others think of him or her. If you say something another doesn't like, you very well won't say that again around this person. You are drawn to others who have learned similar bandwidths of behavior.

The child who deliberately refuses such training learns to rebel. Then the child does exactly what the parents can't tolerate. He or she breaks the unstated care-taking rule. In this situation, however, it is important to understand that the *direction* of the rebellion has been established precisely by the parental training. That is the child rarely rebels in ineffective or random ways.

The result of taking care of the parents is the child isn't encouraged to develop who he or she really is. I put it this way: The child is encouraged to get it right rather than getting it real. Further, he or she learns being real is not the best or is even *bad*. The environment in which the child lives may even be so extreme that the child is encouraged to forget who he or she really is and instead behave in the "right" way--whatever that may be in these parts.

When the child learns how to get it right and take adequate care of the parents, the child is said to be a *good child*.

And the parents may think, "Thank goodness this is not that other one!" That is thank goodness this is not who the child really is.

An entirely different situation occurs when there is an established emotional resonance between the child and his or her parent. In this case the child's feelings will be monitored and considered as important to the parent. Hearing and legitimizing the child's feelings allows the child to feel included. Also if the parent can explain his or her thinking about the discipline being delivered and can also hear the child's thinking about it without being dismissive, the outcome will be a joint enterprise instead of an abusive demand.

The best solution is to allow the child to have a voice in the consequence system that will affect the child. It is also best when the parent is able to take responsibility for his or her own behavior. In such a situation the parent will acknowledge when the limits are primarily for the parent's own benefit.

Each of these things are steps toward removing an authoritarian quality from the consequence system. Any step in this direction will improve the quality of the parent-child emotional bond.

A powerful example of the unheard child may be seen in the following excerpts from Sylvia Plath's poem *Daddy* (1966) where she compares her daddy to a Nazi officer:

Daddy, I have had to kill you.
You died before I had time-------
Marble-heavy, a bag full of God,
Ghastly statue with one grey toe
Big as a Frisco seal

I never could talk to you.
The tongue stuck in my jaw.

It stuck in a barbwire snare.

I have always been scared of *you*,
With your Luftwaffe, your gobbledygoo.

Daddy, you can lie back now.

There's a stake in your fat black heart
And the villagers never liked you.
They are dancing and stomping on you.
They always *knew* it was you.
Daddy, daddy, you bastard, I'm through.

To avoid such outcomes it may seem reasonable to take affairs a step farther and eliminate contingency systems entirely. This is not a good idea as 1) the child needs help in learning how to adjust to the world and other people, 2) a child who faces a constantly neutral parent is robbed of the opportunity to learn coping skills. Such a child is also robbed of the experience of the warmth of human interaction.

Thus it may be seen there is a difference between empathy and obedience. One often hears that children should honor or respect their parents. These things are *earned* by parents. They cannot *demanded*. It is perhaps the biggest irony of all that it is more likely the child will honor and respect an empathic parent than an authoritarian one.

When empathy is not an active consideration, all that remains is behavior. Who is in charge matters a great deal. Who one really is doesn't often matter at all.

14

# YES, BUT

Inevitably when I discuss these ideas with parents, someone sooner or later says: "You just can't let a child run amok!" "We are *responsible* for them, after all." "What about manners?" "What about *society*?"

There are several things to say about this.

First, there is a world of difference between the following two sentences:

    A. "When you do (say) such and such a thing, *you* are bad.

    B. "When you do (say) such and such a thing, *I* freak out.

The difference here is more than the use of "I" words instead of "you" words (which in itself is a good idea). The difference is that in Sentence B I take responsibility for my limitations—which is true. The child is able to see I am trying to cope just as he or she is. I am not a flawless person to be *obeyed*.

Also if I can help the child see there are optional ways to do things, even ones I *can* tolerate, the child grows more effective through the learning of options.

It is important here to point out there is a difference between 1) an emotion and 2) what one does with the emotion. For example, I may be *happy* and *sing*. I may be *happy* and *talk about it.* I may be *happy* and *buy something for a friend.*

*There is no necessary connection between an emotion and what I do with it.*

This principle is often forgotten when the emotion is anger.

A few months ago I was visiting my son and his family who live in Washington D.C. My grandson, Nate, was five years old at the time. I was playing with Nate and his brothers on the floor, and we were building things with many different materials. At one point Nate yelled and smashed everything we had built.

I said, "Nate, are you mad?"

"Mad," he said.

I said, "Do you want to go outside and throw things?"

"Yea," he said.

We went outside and proceeded to have a grand time pelting everything we could find.

Nate got to have his anger, and I tried to help him find a way to deal with it that was harmless and effective.

Miracles happen when a parent says to the child, "I wish I could find a better way to handle situations like this."

Further miracles happen when, after losing it, the parent comes back to the child after regaining sanity and says, "I'm sorry I lost it. I will try to do better."

Why are such messages so powerful? Above all else they demonstrate that the parent is tuned in to the child's feelings. It also admits that parent isn't perfect at handling feelings either. The parent and child are able to join in the effort of trying to do better.

Winnicott (1992) spoke about being a *good enough* parent.

As I said above, if the parent and child aren't reciprocally tuned in to each others' feelings, all that is left to consider is behavior.

*Actually listening to how the child feels without judgment is essential.*

If the parent is tuned into and cares about how the child feels, the child will be induced to tune into and care about how the parent feels. It is not likely such a child will run amok. The questions I get from parents concerned about keeping their children from running amok are likely the same parents who are desperately trying to control their child's behavior—*and*, and the same time, ignoring their feelings.

None of this is to suggest boundaries and limits are not important. They are critical. They are also much more effective if they are clear, discussed, and explained in rational language.

It is important to point out there are two very different kinds of limits.

A. Real world limits

B. Personal limits.

An example of the first is, "If you run in front of the bus, you will lose." An example of the second is, "You can't wear dangly earrings until you are fourteen."

Thus real world limits have to do with existence and survival in the world. These are issues that must be mastered in order to function in life. Personal limits, on the other hand, speak to what the parent can and cannot tolerate. It is routine for parents to get these two categories confused.

Again--from a psychological point of view, how limits are dealt with is just as important as the limits themselves.

The worst possible way to deal with limits is by being authoritarian. Miller (1980) described this. Her list is as follows:

1. Adults are the masters of the dependent child.
2. They determine in godlike fashion what is right and what is wrong.
3. The child is held responsible for the parents' anger.
4. The parents must always be shielded.
5. The child's life-affirming feelings pose a threat to the autocratic adult.
6. The child's will must be "broken" as soon as possible.

7. All this must happen at a very young age so that the child "won't notice" and will therefore not be able to expose the adult.

An essential factor in Miller's list above is that the parents do not listen to the child's genuine feelings nor enter with him or her in cooperative interactions.

In this situation what the child is doing is more important than the relationship between the parent and the child. The behavior alone is the focus.

Such a pattern routinely occurs when the parent has big dreams for the child. Here, the child is induced to follow the parents' way instead of his or her way. For example the child may have her heart set on becoming a cardiologist instead of a housewife. The parents may regard this as crazy or worse: a childhood phase of inflated thinking.

Parental notions of gender could fill their own book. Children are routinely encouraged to belong to a *class* of persons instead of being who they are. Once they have mastered the artifice, they are considered to be a success (see Butler, 1999, Goldner, 2000, Chodorow, 1989, and Flax, 1990, et.al.).

This can be a special problem as gender norms are constantly changing in our culture. This is especially true among different groups of the culture. In such matters parents may be extremely misinformed.

Parents' limits come from their own backgrounds. Further the geneses of these limits are rarely studied. It is therefore often easier for parents to talk about what the child is doing wrong than to talk about what they, as parents, might be doing wrong—or why they think the way they do.

Siegel and Hartzell (2003) wrote impressively about how the parents' thoughts, impulses, and feelings toward the child often say more about the parents than they do about the child. The parents' actions, thus, may seem sensible to the parent but arbitrary and strange to the child.

# EMPATHY AND RESONANCE

Empathy is *feeling with* someone. Compassion is *feeling for* someone. The German word is "Mitleid" which means I am "with your sorrow." That is, I feel it too. The experience is one of a mutual reciprocity of feeling, a *resonance*.

It is axiomatic in attachment research and practice that optimal interactions between parents and infants depend on how the parents "hold the child in their mind." That is, I need to treat you as a person who has your own thoughts and feelings— and these are important. If you, as child, know I am interested in how you think and feel, we will have a different kind of interaction than if I think you are not interested or couldn't care less.

Benjamin (1988) described the kind of interaction in which one person is trying to tune into the thoughts and feelings of another, and the other is trying to tune into the thoughts and feelings of the one. She called this interaction "recognition." That is we recognize each other. Anything other than this, she called "domination."

Thus if I try to dominate you, I erase you. If you try to dominate me, you erase me. The only way we both can be profoundly present is in the mutual resonance of "recognition."

When children are treated in this way, they tend to develop "secure attachment." This allows them to internalize a supportive, resonant parent figure and take it with them. Such a child is less dependent on the external world for maintenance of the self. That is, such a child is less afraid.

Sartre (1964) said:

> I am not a leader, nor do I aspire to become one. Command, obey, it's all one. The bossiest of men commands in the name of another—his father—and transmits the abstract acts of violence which he puts up with. Never in my life have I given an order without laughing, without making others laugh. It is because I am not consumed by the canker of power: I was not taught obedience (p. 13).

It is obvious that the easiest way to abuse another is to fail to care what he or she thinks and feels.

This may be a good way to maintain (resentful, surface) order, but it is the worst possible way to try to have a relationship.

The child who is heard is a lucky child.

It is in this way parents who focus on the outcomes of interactions very often miss the child involved. Such parents are creating outcomes, not caring healthy human beings. The children may be oriented toward achievement, but they will likely experience unending trouble in their relationships.

Similarly if I am spending all my energy trying to be a "good parent," I am likely missing the child. The child doesn't want a good parent. The child wants a genuine parent who listens.

Reedy (2015) reported that the young people he treats told him the best parent was one with his or her "mouth taped shut." Obviously these young people knew a parent who was not tuned into the thoughts and feelings of the young person—but was simply focused on the behavior.

Learning to listen requires one to move beyond his or her own personal experience and to try to imagine the context of another. The other has a different background, different parents, and different circumstances. This is true even if he or she is part of the "same" family. No two children are treated the same way, thought of the same way, have parents with similar experience, &c.

I can begin by imagining how the other person feels and thinks and then move on from this as I hear more from them. One thing I don't want to do, however, is to imagine that their thoughts and feelings are like my own. Or worse: without listening to them claim I know how they feel and what they think. Then they are simply an extension of me.

This is the bane of those who like to give advice. It routinely doesn't occur to such people that the experience and the situation of the other is going to be significantly different.

Such a realization brings us back around to the context.

For someone who basically has had a majority of his or her experience in the same context, that experience will be thought of as the way the world is. It certainly is the way the world has been for this person. For someone who has experienced multiple contexts, however, no one context will be representative of the world. There are simply too many contexts.

The danger in holding the belief that the child thinks as the parent does is sure to fail. If you think about the differences in your experiences this will be obvious. The two of you scarcely live in the same context. Children of rigid, one context parents may fall into this trap, however, because that is what they know. It is how their parents did it. And the parents of their parents.

There is a big difference between these two following pieces of advice.

A. This is the way it is.

B. This has worked for me; you might try it.

Parents who demand their children adopt the same views and behavior as the parents are effectively omitting the child from the equation. In this situation whatever is unique and genuine in the child has to be suppressed.

## SOCIETY AND DEEP BELIEFS

It is routine to hear someone say, "Society demands such and such behavior." It always sounds to me as if in such cases Society is being seen as a giant parent who is a bit like Santa Claus. You know: "He knows if you've been bad or good, so be good for goodness sake."

Society, actually, is an entity made up of people. It is a *reflection* of the people who make it up. It functions more like a giant mirror than it does as a dictatorial agent.

But society, being made up of people who are limited, is itself limited. It might be said the bandwidth of the society is a function of the bandwidths of those who construct it.

Further the establishment and maintenance of society is dependent on *power.* In this situation it is routinely power more than any other factor that is determinate. Power far more than empathic understanding is the political coinage.

It stands to reason that people who were not heard as children are more dependent on social reflection than those who were heard and therefore allowed a more independent development.

A quick visit to a local middle or high school will illustrate this principle quite clearly. For some acceptance into the club becomes a life or death situation. Some are more immune to this influence and instead pursue their own passions.

It is also the case that belonging tends to run along group lines. That is there is a well-documented difference between academic and blue-collar environments. There is also a well-documented difference between rich and poor, and similar subgroups.

The coherence of subgroups can make moving between them extremely difficult.

One's family may be more or less identified with the sub group. For some, the constructs of the subgroup even go so far as to form the basis of the identity of the family. Region, occupation, politics, religious ties, &c may function in this way.

Children who are raised in families like these have been taught to pride themselves on belonging. The question of whether or not one is considered in or out of the group may be of prime importance—not only to the child, but also to the entire family.

Again, such patterns as these tend to minimize who the child is him or herself. Mobility requires the ability to move between contexts, not stand firm and reify one's own context. Couples may pair up based on the fact they both like to do the same things, &c.

It is likely more profitable to consider society as a set of different groups than as a monolith. Academic people, artists, and professional people form a group. Business people form another group. Working and trade people form a group. The disenfranchised form another group. The life of pain and the life of not-pain is not the same life.

It is optimal for the child to be allowed to be who he or she is rather than shaped to fit into an external role. Once the child has a developed a sense of self, fitting will be easier if that option is chosen. But omitting the realization of a developed sense of self leaves a child who is hollow when dissevered from the external context.

The child without a developed sense of self will also find it more difficult to shift contexts. This is poor training for a world that is yearly more complex. That is, one's flexibility increases, as one feels more realized and comfortable in oneself.

In this sense it is healthy to have a developed sense of self apart from where one fits or what one does in society.

The concerns of religion are similar. Religion is not the same thing for those who have a developed independent sense of self than it is for those who only have the religion. This is actually the difference between an internal versus an external sense of identity.

Further the notions of deity that are entertained are significant. Does the deity listen and support or does the deity know what is best for you and issue rules? What happens when you displease the deity?

Or is the deity something like the flow of life? Time? The eternal flux?

Society is constantly evolving. It is steadily moving away from medieval dictatorships and hushed voices to a more genuine consideration of each person.

Authoritarian patterns are increasingly seen as archaic and harmful. Parents who rule their children resemble autocrats. This is also increasingly seen in terms of bosses, teachers, and even project developers.

Autocracy doesn't listen. You listen to it. It matters. You comply.

Children of autocrats very often develop into autocrats themselves. It is all they were allowed to know.

When autocracy is tied up with strong beliefs, it alters the way the child is taught to think. Belief becomes more acceptable as a basis for judgment. There is less need for research and learning. What is important is defending the belief.

What is to some a delight in learning new and even contradictory information is instead seen as a threat and not needed. The excitement at the expanding knowledge base is an excitement for others. Loyalty to certain views is the most important factor.

# BOUNDARIES AND RULES

I have been arguing there is a difference between trying to make a child behave and trying to relate to and love the child. Which focus is central will differ in different households. The focus will also explain volumes about how the parents were raised.

Were my parents more interested in who I am or in how I followed orders? What came to matter most to them had been established in their own childhoods. Still, as with most things, there is a gray area.

There is so much to learn in this world. We all need help. Hopefully it is kind and loving help. It will make the task far easier.

As a child I need to learn about eating, sleeping, hygiene, how to manage strong feelings of anger, hurt, love, fear, and the difficulties inherent in learning to delay gratification.

There is no inherent reason these things need to be taught with anger, force, punishment, or rigid demands. On the other hand, there is no inherent reason I should not learn these things simply because they are distasteful or difficult for me.

A good part of the success or difficulty I will experience in learning will be a function of the ways my parents themselves think about these things as well as the patterns of learning to which they have been exposed.

There are several common ways this training goes wrong.

The first involves confusion between requests and demands. The grammar of a request holds that either a yes or no answer is acceptable. This is what makes it a request.

For example:

"Please change chairs."

"Bite me."

"Okay."

This is okay because "Bite me" (here used as a grammatical equivalent of "No") is acceptable in this case.

If, however, I say "Please change chairs," and "No" is not an acceptable answer, then I am making a demand.

Demands must be obeyed. Requests allow for a decision.

Obviously the more requests a family uses, the better people will feel about being in the family. This is true as they are allowed to have a voice.

It is not uncommon, however, to run into parents who make a request:

"Freddy please take out the garbage."

Freddy, reading the grammar correctly, says:

"Bite me."

The parent then changes the request into a demand. What Freddy learns is that a request is simply a cheap prelude to a demand. Thus, everything becomes a demand.

Requests and demands are very different kinds of things. It is important to know this difference and use each appropriately. Neither one, by itself, will be optimal in all situations.

A second way training goes wrong is when the parent confuses the grammar of "I" and "you." Popular psychology treatments have taught us the wisdom of using "I statements" instead of "you statements."

It is common for a parent to say:

"You made me mad!"

This is *always* false.

It really is too bad the child can't say:

"You're the one who is responding with anger. Don't put this on me. Go see a therapist."

The child would be correct. Clarity requires seeing the child did or said what he or she did. The parent responded with anger (among several options.)

How I respond is how *I* respond. The response came from me, not you. Also, I have options about how I might respond. I might, for example, say:

"I can't stand what you are doing. I think I'm going to go insane. I am unable to cope with what you are doing, &c."

This is a much healthier response, primarily because it is true. Not realizing this truth, the parent is likely teaching the child to take care of him or her—and be responsible for the parent's feelings as well.

"It is my fault you are mad."

This, too, is *always* false.

Such a situation may lead to one of the great moments in helping a child. That is, it is important that the parent *own* and take *accountability* for his or her own feelings and behavior.

"I am the one who is mad. I am the one who doesn't know what to do."

In making such a statement, I acknowledge I am not a perfect person or a perfect parent. In fact, I am having as much trouble coping as is the child.

I do what I do, and the child does what he or she does. We both have feelings. It is how we respond to each other's feelings that will determine the nature of our interaction.

When we are tuned into each other's feelings, we are taking care of each other.

A third way training goes wrong is when the parent feels compelled to consider every thought, feeling, and behavior of the child as either "right" or "wrong."

Here, the parent sets him or herself up as a judge. No matter what the child thinks, feels, or does will be judged by the parental supreme awareness of what is right and what is wrong.

I had a patient who had a recurring dream. He was hauled before "the great judge." The judge sat fifty feet above him behind a massive desk. The judge would bang his gavel and unfurl a huge scroll over the front edge of the desk. This scroll listed all the faults and shortcoming of the patient. Then the judge would lean his scowling, be-speckled face across the front of his desk and say in sonorous tones, "J-o-s-e-p-h."

It doesn't take a great deal of imagination to think about how this (very accomplished and successful adult man) was raised.

Obviously a parent is not a world-class authority on what is right or wrong. But that is not how it comes across to the child. Furthermore, such a parent routinely confuses:

"You did something bad."

"You are bad."

The first statement has to do with guilt, whereas the second has to do with shame. Such feelings, aside from being difficult to manage, are wounding to the child.

Also it is routine for parents to go on and confuse "You did something bad" and (therefore) "You are bad."

Here the only possible redemption is to be flawless, that is unassailable—no criticism possible.

And if only perfection is good enough, the parent doesn't understand what it is to be a *human being*.

But the bigger error is that such a parent is so focused on how things need to be (should be) that he or she loses contact with the child and only focuses on the outcome.

Typically what I think of as good and bad is the result of how I was raised—how my parents thought of these things. It is far from being an eternal truth. The next-door neighbor might not agree.

A fourth way training goes wrong is when the parent notices all the child's "bad" behavior and unwittingly ignores the "good." He or she may not be aware he or she is doing this.

In this situation, the only time the child may be noticed is when he or she is doing something considered bad. When he or she does things considered good, he or she is ignored.

The opposite of love is not hate. If I can't get you to love me, I will try to get you to hate me. Then you have to be involved with me. The opposite of love and hate is *indifference*. I will do whatever I can to avoid that.

It is important to reward what the child does well and help the child improve what he or she does not do well.

A fifth way training goes wrong is when parents use punishment for what does not go well.

Punishment as a consequence has many things wrong with it. Perhaps the main thing wrong with it is that it introduces strong emotional reactions into the situation that are difficult to manage and may be long lasting.

Options to punishment include:

The first and foremost option involves *attitude*. If I am trying to frighten or hurt the child, that is a different approach than trying to help the child. If I am trying to frighten or hurt the child, I need to see a therapist myself. Yesterday.

Second, I need to make sure I am trying to help the child instead of helping myself. Trying to train the child to be the least possible trouble, so I can maximize my time away from the child, is abusive in a subtle, long lasting way. Here, how I hold the child in my mind is that his or her life should be in the service of helping me.

Third, consequences that are delivered *neutrally* have the best outcomes. Consequences are not de-

signed to be punitive. They are simply consequences. For example:


"If you get into bed at bedtime, I will read you
a story."


If the child does everything but going to bed at
the appropriate time, he or she loses the opportunity to have a story. It's that simple. No lecture. No
discussion of how bad the child is. No anger necessary. It is even possible to empathize with the
child over losing the story. But the consequence
remains.

The best consequences are those that are discussed beforehand in a neutral emotional time.
The child needs to give input. His or her feelings
need to be considered.

Children whose feelings are heard and who get
to participate in the consequence system tend to
develop *internal boundaries* that operate even
when *external boundaries* are missing. If the child
is simply ordered about, he or she will only develop reliance on external boundaries. *This* is the
child who is in danger of running amok.

If the child has a consequence (i.e., loses the story), he or she may say, "I hate you!" As a parent I can say, "I know you are mad. I don't blame you. Maybe tomorrow you will be able to have a story."

I can even add, "I love you."

Again, it is critical that the next thing the child does well is rewarded.

Another option to punishment is the procedure known as *time out*. Here the child is removed from the opportunity to respond.

For example if the child throws his or her plate of food on the floor, time out may be appropriate.

In this procedure, it is best to have a time out place. This is a place used for time out alone. If such a place is not available, a time out chair can be used. The chair is best in its own place, away from the other goings on in the house.

The child is required to sit in the chair for the duration of the time out. I never allowed time out to extend longer than five minutes with my son Anthony. No other behavior is allowed during the time out. There is no response to comments on the part of the child. The idea is the child has been removed from the action for five minutes.

That's it. No post time out lectures. The child did the crime and has now done the time. It's over. Again this works best when there is a neutral emotional attitude involved. It is a *consequence*, not a *punishment*.

Another option to punishment in certain circumstances is *talking through* of the situation. This can only be done effectively by a parent who is not blaming the child, who is not furious with the child, and who is really trying to help the child learn how to do it better.

In all these instances, changed behavior or doing it better needs to be noticed and rewarded adequately.

Finally, the parent is wise to admit his or her own struggle with feelings and behaviors. This kind of parent does better than one who represents him or herself as flawless, all knowing, and perfect—that is, as someone other than he or she is.

And when the parent does make a mistake, it is wise to acknowledge this and apologize for it.

The child knows he or she is the child and the parent is the parent. A loving parent is far preferable than one who sees his or her role as being in charge.

It is important to point out again that the opposite of autocracy is not an anything goes, out of control context where the child is allowed to run amok. Amok is not a natural state. An amok child may be a reflection of an amok parent, one who does not have a meaningful relationship with the child.

# MINDING THE CHILD

How the parent holds the child in his or her mind will help shape how the child thinks of him or herself in return.

A colleague told me a story of one of her patients, a beautiful teenaged girl. During the course of their treatment, the girl admitted she had significant same sex attraction, and that this had been the case for a long time. The girl was tired of living in the closet and realized a life of duplicity was not in her best interests.

She wanted to tell her very religious parents about her truth, but she was afraid of how they might react. She asked her therapist (my colleague) if she could bring the parents into session with her and tell them in the presence of the therapist. The therapist was fine with this option.

At the next session the girl brought in her parents, but she was too frightened to tell them. She discussed all manner of things until she was able to blurt out: "I'm gay. I have been forever."

At this the mother looked shocked and displeased, and the father said: "We'd rather you were dead."

The colleague, who was a highly skilled and experienced psychologist, said that it took her several days to realize: that is what the parents had been telling the girl all along.   They had never really had her "in mind."

This incident reminds me of a paragraph from the German poet Rilke (1949) in which he describes an old birthday.

> ...hardly is one awake when somebody shouts outside that the cake hasn't arrived yet; or one hears something break as the presents are being arranged on the table in the next room; or somebody comes in and leaves the door open, and one sees everything before one should have seen it. That is the moment when something like an operation is performed on one: a brief but atrociously painful incision. But the hand that does it is experienced and steady. It is quickly over. And scarcely has it been survived, when one no longer thinks about oneself; one must rescue the birthday, watch the others, anticipate their mistakes, and confirm them in the illusion that they

are managing everything admirably...They contrive to come in with parcels of some sort that [seem to be] destined for other people...Talent was really necessary only when someone had taken pains and, important and kind, brought one a joy, and one saw even at a distance that it was a joy for somebody quite different...(p 129).

Here the child saves the family and enables it all to come out as the family wanted—even to the point about being gracious about a gift he did not want, a gift for "someone else."

Last year when I returned from a trip to Prague, I brought my grandson Nate a Czech bank note.

"Here, Nate, I brought you some Czech money!"

He looked at this and said:

"Jami, that's not fun for me."

He did *not* protect me, but, instead, gave me the gift of his real self.

If the child is not admired for being who he or she really is, the child will have to find a way to survive. He or she will have to undergo Rilke's "atrociously painful incision." Like a child who is required to sit through all those endless family dinners, it will slowly occur to him or her how little the others had him or her in mind. In a very real sense the child was not allowed to be there at all.

It is significant that when the child described by Rilke above transitioned into being an adult, he had to dissever himself from his childhood and the people in it.

> I am inclined to believe that the
> strength of his transformation lay in
> his no longer being anybody's son
> (Ibid., p. 162)

It is quite amazing how many parents think they know their children but have never asked them, "Who are you?" Or maybe better: "Do you dare tell me who you are?" Such parents simply assume they know who the child is.

Everyone around the child assumes they know who the child is. The teacher, the neighbor, the preacher, the aunts and uncles, everyone. Each one of these people develops a construction of the child and routinely assumes it is correct.

They all, if you will, hold a different child in their minds. It is this range of views the good child has to protect and support. That is the family way. That is how we do it around here. That's "who we are."

Not the least of these surround characters are the parents of the mother and father—that is the people to whom the parents are children. How do they see the child? How do they see the child's parents?

In such arrangements there are layers and layers of rules. Some of these rules are conscious. Some are unconscious. Some are acknowledged. Some are denied. The child is rarely in a position to challenge any of these rules.

It is not surprising that the child becomes confused, and childhood is largely reduced to an effort to avoid negative consequences instead of it being an effort to enjoy life and oneself.

Obedience can become the number one imperative. And as Benjamin (above) argued, obedience erases the self.

# THE GOOD CHILD GROWS UP

Adolescence is typically the time when children begin to shift their identifications from the parents to the peer group. That is, they begin to move from the home into the "outside" world.

This can be a perilous time for the good child in at least three ways.

The child who has been taught to obey and take care of the parents at his or her own expense is caught in a powerful cross-fire. In Middle School the in-group becomes established and serves as a replacement for the parents.

A child without a developed sense of self will find him or herself tossed between competing groups. Not having a sense of self upon which to stand, such a child must either remain steadfastly lined up with his or her parents or must find a group to join.

The child's *identity* requires this. Without a developed real self, the group functions like the identity. One shifts the skills one learned taking care of one's parents to taking care of the group.

If I have a developed sense of self, I have a "me" before I align with anybody. If I don't have a "me" other than a "care taking me," that is the only kind of me I have. The rest is vestigial.

If I have not been able to develop a real self, I must fit in with others to have an identity. Being without them is worse than being lonely. It is almost to not be.

Of course I am presenting this in black or white fashion to make the point clear. In reality there are all sorts of shades of grey.

A danger at this juncture is that the child without a developed sense of self *will* run amok. Such a child may feel so wounded by the way his or her childhood happened, he or she may want to use new found power to "stick it" to the parents. That is, to do precisely what the parents can't tolerate.

I may get tattoos and have a stud placed in my nose. I may become a substance abuser or addict. I may drop out of school and live on the street.

Fitting into the group may become a life-long project. It is, in effect, all I know how to do. The group will be highly important to me, as it is my grounding. Without the group, I fear I am nothing.

I may actually be of great value to the group, and I may be able to make significant contributions. My contributions, however, will most likely be "within the bandwidth" contributions. I will not likely be the one to rock the boat with new "out of the bandwidth" contributions. I will be the one who survives by taking care of people.

The problem with this sort of adjustment is that the child is still left out. That is, the undeveloped self of the (now) adult needs to find a way to emerge in addition to his or her developed care-taking and pleasing abilities.

The requirement to remain beholden to child-hood rules will likely be unconscious, though it may be observed by others. I only allow myself to go so far.

I also likely have a strong internalized parent that is critical of what I do. This internalized parent may be a recurring thought that I have not done well enough. It criticizes everything I do, and I routinely end up on the short end of the stick—re-gardless of the real world value of what I do.

This internalized critic will be as paramount in my life as my parents were in my childhood.

Further, I will need to do whatever I can to please it. This will turn out to be an endless and futile task, however, as the internalized critic will never be satisfied. It will only be mollified if I take sufficient care of it.

In a sense I will be married to it. It will be prior in all my interactions and in what I do. I will be no more free of it than I was of my parental injunctions.

This situation will inevitably create relationship problems for at least two reasons.

The first is that my primary psychological allegiance will be to this inner critic and to the necessity that I try to please it. Thus I won't be able to have a primary allegiance with my partner or others—including my children. There will always be boundaries I am unable to cross. This will limit my capability in significant ways.

The second, and far more critical, problem will be that I won't have a developed sense of self to bring to the relationship. Yes, I will be able to take care of others and to please (as long as they don't demand things too much at odds with my inner critic), but I won't be able to function as a real self.

Again, I will strive to get things right instead of striving to get them real.

And the cycle will begin again.

It is routine for parents to focus on what the child does and not focus on who the child is. Such a child learns his or her worth is contingent upon what he or she does. Do well and you are a good kid. Do poorly and you are a bad kid. One's identity depends on what one does, not upon who one is.

The critical inner voice is constantly monitoring what such a person does and finding fault with it. In extreme cases only perfection of performance will do. Anything assailable is bad. The child can never win at this equation.

# I'VE DONE EVERYTHING WRONG—IS THERE ANY HOPE FOR ME?

Probably.

It is certainly worth a try.

The most difficult cases will be the ones in which children have had their real thoughts and feelings outlawed and instead treated like objects.

Many parents are able to grow psychologically and come to new understandings and feelings. These are parents who have been able to experience contexts different from those they knew as children—and perhaps even those they knew as adults.

Things change. Having children changes us. Virtually everything changes. It is not unusual for parents to become amazed at the power of the feelings they have for the child. Parenthood may be deeply sobering. One thing is sure: the context of one's life with a child in it is a very different context than one's life without a child.

For some it is a chance to live one's own childhood over again and to try to eliminate what was wrong before.

There is also the issue of time. The world of one's childhood is rarely the world of one's adulthood. The culture is in constant flux. The Internet, for example, has changed practically everything.

We grow and see from different perspectives. Things are not the way they used to be. We must adjust, sometimes hugely. The world of our childhood is not the world of today. We can, for example, cure things against which we once felt powerless.

Knowledge is exploding in scope. We are rapidly learning things never before known in the history of the world. We also are able to benefit from efforts of past generations. We have more perspectives.

We may enter therapy and develop a clearer picture of who we are. We may also develop awareness of the factors that figure in the way we think, feel, and react. We may review where we have been and what we have done. Acceptance of who we are may lead us to further development.

These efforts may give us new perspectives and abilities in dealing with our children. If we have made a mess of things, we may be able to discover how this happened.

Even more significantly, our children may enter therapy. There, our influence and treatment of them will be examined. They will be able to understand more about themselves and also develop greater awareness of us. What hurt them will likely become clear, and they can help us understand that as well.

We may divorce, and the child's matrix as well as ours may face a dramatic shift. This change in context may reveal new possibilities as well as new requirements.

Our circumstances as a family may dramatically change. What we used to have, we may no longer have. We may socially advance significantly. Illness, accidents, changes of location, deaths in the family, loss of employment, dramatic advancements, all these are ongoing factors of life.

And, of course, we all age. Some of us become wiser. Some of us do not. Age and experience may mellow us, or it may create more problems. Age brings differing perspectives along with differing challenges. It brings new contexts.

We may learn more. We may go back to school or meet someone who teaches us a great deal. We may meet new friends who do things dramatically differently--with dramatic results.

Our children change contexts, and we have to deal with that. They grow. They change schools and peer groups. They learn new things--things we don't know. They become more independent and less reliant on our input. They develop their own sexuality along with ways to manage that.

Children marry. We find ourselves entwined with a whole different family. Our role as parents shifts dramatically. Our children become parents themselves and themselves find ways to interact with their children that may be different from our ways. The new family begins to move in its own direction.

The list of changes go on and on. At each point there is an opportunity for growth. We might say changes change. It is our only constant.

# ANGER

As we all have limits, all of us become angry. How we manage our anger is a significant factor in our lives both personally and interpersonally. It is also a central part of parent-child interactions.

At its base, there is a difference between 1) the *feeling* of anger and 2) what we *do* with that anger. The feeling itself may be a rather singular sort of thing, but there are almost an infinite number of things that might be done with it.

Anger usually has a flash reaction during which one is highly aroused. This is the dangerous time. When the flash reaction has subsided, rational thought is again possible. This is the reason for the old "count to ten" (before you say anything) rule.

One thing to do with anger (after the flash) is to talk about it. Another is to own it. For example, "I'm having a hell of a time trying to manage my feelings when you do that." This says 1) I am angry and 2) I am trying to manage it.

Contrast such a statement with, "You made me mad." Here I transfer the responsibility for the anger to you, and I imply that without your terrible behavior I would be fine and dandy.

This is never true. Without your terrible behavior I would still be the limited person I am.

Shifting of responsibility for anger is common in parent-child interactions. Also common is another troublesome pattern: under the table anger and double messages.

This is another way to avoid taking responsibility for one's feelings. Such a thing is accomplished when the parents are smiling and proper over the table, but they are upset and angry under the table.

"Can I go play with Debbie?"

"Sure you can go," (uttered with the tone of "If you take one step I will kill you.")

When the child protests and says, "You never let me do anything," the parent can deny the under the table message and only admit the over the table message.

"I said you could go, and you attack me!" (What a screwed up, ungrateful child you are.)


These techniques establish the fact that the parent's displeasure is the child's fault. It is the child who is the problem. Such a fact may become enshrined in how the family thinks about and treats each other. The child becomes, in the language of therapy talk, the "identified problem" (the "IP").

Family therapists are always pointing out that the IP is routinely the most responsible member of the family. He or she is taking the heat so the other members can be okay.

A working sense of empathy would ruin the above pattern. If the family members were trying to resonate with how each other feels, they could not play such a game.

A year or so ago a friend sent me the following photo he had gotten from the Internet. It shows rather clearly different pressures that can exist in a family. My favorite.

Simmonds (2002) studied the aggression of adolescent girls. Girls, she argued, are trained to hide their aggression instead of being open about it as boys are allowed to do. The world of adolescent girls becomes a vast under the table war field where little is as it seems.

Here again, when the focus is not on empathic interaction, the focus shifts to power and achievement. Empathy is cast aside. Scapegoating becomes routine.

Even beyond adolescence we as people are constantly required to spend a great deal of time to take care of angry people. When these angry people also have narrow, rigid bandwidths, interaction becomes exceedingly difficult.

Such people were routinely parented the same way they behave around others. The "gold" passes along, as it were. These people also become parents and discipline their children the only way they know how: they make the child responsible for the parents anger.

There was a very funny cartoon in the New Yorker magazine a few years ago. It showed a house that had burned to the ground. A whiff of smoke was still rising. In front of the house there was a mother, father, and a child. The caption under the cartoon was: We're not mad at you Johnny; we're only mad at what you did.

No parent has the unlimited resources to raise a child or have a relationship without becoming angry. How that anger is managed will play a large part in the development of the character of the child and the health of the relationship.

Homes where the parents are good and the child is bad are toxic environments. They are, in short, as damaging as homes in which everyone appears to be good, but there is no empathy.

I worked with a colleague who was known to be friendly and pleasant to people's faces, but when their backs were turned, she could be hostile and attacking of these same people. She, in short, could not be trusted. Sooner or later she stabbed everyone she knew.

She once asked me to talk to her (instead of others) if I wanted to know anything about her. If I did this, she would surely have contorted what she told me to make herself look good. The net upshot was that one couldn't talk to her or trust her. Yet throughout this time she appeared sunny and friendly.

Such duplicity is crazy-making in a parent. A good rule to remember is that *the anger comes across whether it goes across the top of the table or under the table*. It is simply not true we can hide our feelings—unless, that is, we are hiding them from someone who doesn't wish to see them.

Also your anger says more about you than it does about the other.

## THE HOME TEMPLATE

As children we typically begin our lives at home. This is our first environment, our first context. How the people are at home is my first sense of how people are in general. What the circumstances of home are is my first sense of how circumstances are, &c.

If my mother is unwelcoming, I will first learn that others and women are unwelcoming. If my father is autocratic, I will first learn that others and men are autocratic. If the parents must always win, I first learn that others need to win.

I will also develop a way of being in such a context. I may be calm or hyper. I may be resilient or touchy. I may be adventurous or timid, &c.

The qualities of this environment will become internalized as my first sense of how the world is. For example I bought my four-year-old grandson a Cookie Monster doll and gave it to him.

"I brought you a present; it's the Cookie Monster," I said.

"He only eats cookies."

The child looked at me and said:

"Doesn't he need a balanced diet?"

"No," I said, "He just eats cookies!"

The child had never heard of such a thing. This was clearly out of his context and experience.

These examples are rather obvious. But how about families in which feelings are discussed routinely as opposed to families where feelings are not discussed at all? This is akin to families in which reading is routine as opposed to families where reading never occurs.

The two most important elements families can provide for the stability and mental well-being of the child are that: 1) the child feels *safe,* and 2) the child feels *welcome.*

Parental limits can curtail the range of acceptance and thus unwittingly compromise the child's feelings in these areas.

Surely the two worst historical candidates for military school were the poets Shelly and Rilke. Yet both were sent there in what must count as among the greatest empathic failures of all time.

Parents who are fearful of everything tend to raise children who are likewise fearful. Parents who are socially gregarious tend to raise similar children. There are business families, artistic families, sports families, religious families, &c. There are families who are unable to deal with rebellion and angry children.

In any family, it is the quality of the emotional connection between the parents and the child that is most critical. Two-way, open communication of as many thoughts and feelings as possible insures an optimal baseline context.

Parents who give their children every sort of material thing to make up for a lack of emotional richness are likely to raise deeply resentful children.

In our culture people routinely become parents without considering anything other than themselves. This includes not learning about mastering what will maximize their child's mental health and coping abilities. The result is children often get raised the way their parents were raised.

Either that, or the new parents find the child an intolerable burden. The child is then emotionally shunned and isolated. His or her voice is not heard. He or she is thought to be, by definition, a problem.

Parents may be drunk, coked-out, in jail, doing prostitution out of the home—squaller and loud music may be blaring twenty-four-seven. Dinner may sometimes be available, sometimes not. Doctor and dentist visits may be nonexistent. Hygiene may be anywhere along the scale.

Some parents may provide opulent surroundings but are themselves essentially emotionally absent.

The catch is that it is critical how the parent holds the child in his or her mind. That is where the child will start. That will be who he or she will think he or she is.

# THREATS AND CONTINGENCIES

When behavior occurs, there are always consequences to that behavior. Basically a consequence may be positive, negative, or neutral. But behavior does not occur in a vacuum.

Consequences can be established in advance. It may be a family rule, for example, that breaking knickknacks result in a time out. It is important, when such a rule is established, that it apply to all members of the family.

In graduate school I heard of a device called the Sunday Box. This was a cardboard box, painted, say, red, with the name Sunday Box written on it. The logic of the device is that anything that is found laying around out of place will be tossed in the Sunday Box, and it can't be gotten out until Sunday.

Usually by the end of the first day, all of little Michael's toys, socks, and pajamas are in the Sunday Box. This goes rather well until Daddy comes home from work in a foul mood, two martini's to the wind, slumps down in the sofa, and throws his car keys on the coffee table.

Swift as a speeding bullet Michael swoops in from the bedroom and throws daddy's keys in the Sunday Box. What now? Do the rules hold equally for all? Are the rules only for Michael while the parents can do anything they choose? Just what is the message here?

Contingencies are best when they are clear and not too strict. Children, after all, have to have space to learn. It is also best when consequences are unemotionally monitored and adjudicated.

This is to say consequences needn't be accompanied by anger. They may be accompanied by a desire to help.

An obvious option to consequences is the use of threats. These are all too common in families. Whereas consequences can be worked out in calm ahead of time, threats routinely are made in the heat of some moment on the spot.

> "If you don't get back in your chair
> by the time I count to three, there
> will be no more food for the rest of
> the day!"

It is, of course, routine for children to ignore such comments as well as equally routine for parents not to follow through on them.

Two hours later when the child really is hungry and crying for something to eat, it is given.

I am not arguing for hard-ass parenting here, the point is that consequences tend to be more effective than threats because they are rational and (hopefully) dispassionately maintained. Threats, on the other hand, are inherently emotional, punitive in nature, and poorly monitored.

There was one rule in my house when I was a parent. It was: *Everybody's feelings get to count.*

# TOUCH, HAPPINESS, AND SOLEMNITY

It is critical not to omit the importance of touch in the child's life. By this I mean warm, welcoming, accepting touch. Back rubs. Floor rolls. We are creatures of touch as much as we are creatures of thought. When touch is working between a parent and a child the empathy of their feelings becomes apparent.

"Can I sit by you?"

"Can I have a hug?"

Including easy and welcome touch in the interaction makes touch an integral part of the exchange. This is healthy grounding for future intimate exchanges.

Further, warm, welcoming touch should be available all the time, not only when the child is being "good." The behavior might not be adored, but the child is. What is adored, in other words, is *who the child is.* That is, the child is not only adored, because of what he or she does.

Learning that I am lovable only when I do the right thing makes my status as a human being uncertain and dependent upon what I do. This is called "contingent evaluation" and leads to all sorts of psychological problems.

The child needs to learn he or she is *lovable period.*

These things were apparent in Harlow's (1971) series of experiments with baby monkeys. Infants deprived of maternal warmth and nurturing were heartbreakingly crippled in many ways. Even minor interruptions in this had significant effects.

In extreme cases relations between parents and children may become so strained there is no happiness experienced by the family at all.

The child needs to experience a free range of emotions to find out how to manage them. A family that is only happy is not a real family. This is also true of a family that is always angry. Such relationships are actually part-families.

The missing parts matter. It is not a good thing for mommy or daddy to get mad and shut down for the entire weekend. None of these messages are helpful for the child.

People who genuinely like to be around each other—happy or not—are having powerfully shaping experiences. If, further, everyone can be heard the results are optimum.

It is also important these experiences are genuine, not feigned. Simply saying, "Isn't this fun?" doesn't make it fun.

"Come on; we're going to visit Aunt Edna."

Groan.

"Aunt Edna is a nice person."

Groan.

Here the child is not being heard, and his or her feelings are being ignored. Clearly the parent wants to visit Aunt Edna, not the child. Again, the child is being asked to take care of the parent.

If this is a situation in which it is critical for the parent to visit Aunt Edna and there is no one to look after the child, other techniques could be found.

"What sort of reward would make it worth your while to visit Aunt Edna with me *for a half hour?*

"Could you come with me and play in Aunt Edna's yard?"

"I have to stop by Aunt Edna's place to pick up an item I need. Please come with me and then we can get ice cream."


The point is the child needs to be able to share in the experience and gain some happiness from it. It can't be all about the parent.

In similar fashion, though in a different context, it is important the child see the parent having genuine feelings, including solemnity. This shows the child there are things bigger than the parent, bigger than anyone. The solemnity in question is a genuine experience of the sacred. *It is not merely going to church.* Going to church is typically a *ritual*. Experiencing the sacred is a *direct experience.*

The sacred need not even be religious. It may be an experience of the vastness and power of eternity and time. It may be a place. It could even be a day of the year.

We might say the sacred is an emotional truth as opposed to a factual truth. Things that are sacred are the things most meaningful to us.  The sacred is *found*. It is not *forced*.  There are people who avoid it, who say they don't understand it, or who confuse it with religious dogma.

The sacred is that from which we came and that to which we expire. It is, if you will, the *ground* of life. The "force-field."

Children have this experience as a matter of course. It is wise to also consider their experience of the sacred and what deeply matters to them (i.e., *The Velveteen Rabbit)*—and protect it as they do. This allows the child to be more present.

It is not wise to force parental views onto children for all the reasons given above.  Then the child must essentially obey or rebel. The sacred is different. It is little, and quiet, and kept in a special place.

It moves mountains.

# THE NEW WORLD

Our children were *not* born into the same world we were. They have different parents than we did. They live in a different time. The pressures on them are different. Schools are different. The culture is different.

Also the pace of life is far different. The demands to adjust are far greater. The world has shrunk even farther. Being able to manage diversity is widely greater.

Raising a child to fit into the world of our own childhoods is not doing them a favor. The world they face is not one thing. It is many things. In order to survive countries must pull together. Our cities are filled with people unlike us--and we have to get along with them.

There is no longer one right way.

As if there ever were. There is no longer one right point of view. There are multiple points of view, and they all need to be heard. To be included. Society is trying to find a way to be more inclusionary and less exclusionary, more tolerant of difference.

How do we help our children prepare for such a world? Can we?

It would seem there are several things we could do.

Developing home environments that encourage a working sense of empathy is a good place to begin. Children who are able to consider each other's feelings are better equipped to work with different kinds of people than their less empathic peers. Well-being must be emotional as well as physical.

Children who are raised in an environment of reciprocal empathy are better equipped to realize environments where reciprocal empathy is lacking, such as the climate of the mean girls in school. Such children also learn an alternative to an emotionally barren life of endless struggle after achievement.

Children can be taught the importance of difference by being asked to consider different points of view. They can be helped to experience different contexts. Parents can introduce them to different kinds of people. Children can be helped to learn about different customs, cultures, and ways of seeing the world.    Language learning might be stressed.

These things are best accomplished when the parents undertake to develop these abilities as well instead of simply demanding the child do so.  This requires parents to "walk the walk" instead of simply "talking the talk."

The development of flexibility is important.  Jobs change, relationships change, locales change, economic circumstances can change--often dramatically, world events change rapidly, and the demands one faces constantly change.  Coping skills are increasingly tested.

Persons who are able to stand on their own feet and make considered adjustments are more likely to prosper than persons who only know how to fit into a limited number of structures.  Being unable to think and act on one's own is an enormous advantage.

Children whose voices and feelings matter are never taught their feelings and voices don't matter.  Such children are not excluded and taught, thereby, to be powerless.  Children who are helped interacting with others are not left to be clumsy or shy.

In the new world truth has been "de-centered." That is there is no longer considered to be one truth as was the case in Enlightenment thinking. Truth can no longer be dissevered from its context. This means what you see depends upon where you stand. Truths are truths within contexts. This makes them akin to words, which are meaningful within contexts.

The context matters.

Rigid adherence to one sort of truth is actually seen as rigid adherence to one context--to the exclusion of all others. In the new world all contexts matter. It is an *inclusive* rather then an *exclusive* world. Success in such a world requires children to have the ability to adapt to rather constantly shifting contexts. Rigidity becomes an impediment.

It is in this way authoritarianism becomes a problem. When only those in charge have a voice the benefit of many voices is lost. That is to say many voices are excluded. As a collective we lose their input and are therefore held to narrow perspectives.

Every voice, every child, has something to say--something that needs hearing. Further those voices are constantly changing with the evolving culture.

It is more important for the child to be a *flexible* child than to be an *obedient* child.

# UNIQUENESS

It seems obvious to say every child is his or her unique being. No two children have the same parents, the same experiences, the same environments, the same struggles. This is true even if the two children come from the "same" family.

Solutions that worked for someone else will likely not be optimal for the child. Solutions that were used on parents when they were young are not likely to be optimal for the child. Statistical norms, how other children behave in the neighborhood, opinions of well meaning others, and comparisons between siblings are not likely to be optimal.

What is optimal is a consideration of the child in his or her own context. The child's voice must be significantly heard. It is important to discover and love what is unique in the child. It is also important to help the child find his or her own adjustment to the world around him or her.

Not all children are destined for football, the Ivy League, motherhood, the corporate boardroom, taking over the family gas station, family life, &c., &c.

The parent's view of the child comes from the parent's context, which is different from the child's context in many ways. Again, the parents had different parents than the child. They had to fit into different contexts than the child. They grew up in a different time than the child. They (often) grew up in a different place, in different circumstances, with different peers, and different sets of expectations.

Some parents were heard and encouraged to find the things that worked for them--and were then supported and encouraged to pursue those things. Other parents were not heard and were expected to fit into parental desires for them. These are not similar parents.

Some children are exposed to multiple contexts. Some are restricted to very few. Some were helped to find the magic in reading, music, technical inventions, athletics, and the language itself. Others were largely spared these dimensions. Some were able to find the magic in other people. Others tried as best they could to avoid other people.

All these children go to school and sit together in a room. Is it the "same" room? They are induced to play with each other. They come home with joys, fears, struggles and stories to tell. Some need a space to get away.  Some need to play together. Some need to talk.  Some need to crash.

Are the kids included in family planning?  Do they get asked what they want to do on the weekend?  Do they get helped with their homework questions?  Do they get over-helped?  Are they put to work, because the parent needs it, believes in it? Are the children asked?  Do they get to wear their spontaneously outrageous outfits?  Do they not? Are there important experiences in their life that don't require stuff?

Is there time for just the kids?  Is there time when the kids get to lead?  Is there adequate reward *according to the child* for what the parents want the child to do?  Are there adequate rewards for creativity? Empathic interaction? Down time?

Hopefully consequences are explained clearly, completely, and rationally, allowing for input from the child.  Opportunities for rewards are spelled out clearly, completely, and rationally.  There is adequate time to simply hang out.

The child knows he or she is loved *simply for being who he or she is*.

Perhaps most importantly the parents tolerate learning who the child really is—and help the child embrace, maximize, and love that person.

## THE FIX

In order for the good child to be helped, he or she (at any age) must find a way to recognize the problem and find the courage to approach it.

It will be essential this person find a context that is other than his or her childhood. Often, this involves therapy. The therapist must not have the same wound, or the wound of the patient may go unrecognized. Further it will likely not be easy to tease out.

The good child has learned to restrict his or her behavior to that which another can tolerate. This approach will also be used on the therapist.

As the patient talks, the therapist will be able to note the ways the patient feels inadequate or worthless. This will likely be puzzling to the therapist, because such ways of being are not considered inadequate or worthless by the therapist.

*It is this mismatch that leads to the improvement.*

The significant therapeutic exchange will be between a patient who operates under a cloud of criticalness and a therapist who does not.

The childhood will be explored, and it will become clear that the parents had their own limitations. The fact the parents could not stand any behavior, thought, or feeling outside their bandwidth will become known.

It will be noticed the patient's internalized critic duplicates the actions and opinions of the parents. In this way it will be seen the patient has unconsciously smuggled his or her childhood into adulthood. He or she is held prisoner of that childhood. Its tyranny persists.

That the patient has an unconscious allegiance to the internalized critic that was similar to the allegiance he or she had with the parent will allow for the realization that the patient dare not disobey the critic. This will be true for the same reason the child did not dare disobey the parent.

In other words, it remains imperative that the inner critic be obeyed instead of the patient developing a real self.

These realizations will likely be difficult for the patient to achieve, as the internalized critic is loud and seen as correct. It has rarely been seriously challenged. The internalized critic will surely take on the therapist in the same way it takes on any threat—by attack.

It will fall to the therapist to be a caring, empathic parent figure who supports the patient while he or she discovers a real sense of self—and then take the first frightening steps to be that person.

This stance on the part of the therapist will have to be genuine, or the effect will not adequately occur. The treatment will simply turn into another form of the "don't be who you are" game.

There is routinely considerable pain involved in rescuing the good pleasing self from its childhood. The entire childhood may have to be moved on from—as one would move from one country to another.

Though "surface" moves like this are not complete cures in any stretch of the imagination, still such moves *do* shift the context. In a new context people will respond to one differently. Different things will likely be valued, &c. One will play a different part in the new context from that played in the old.

The value of experiencing new and different contexts cannot be overstated. This is the case as an internal view and an external view are never the same. If one knows only one's original context, one has nothing with which to compare that context. That is, there is no not-original context to demonstrate a difference. Difference and contrast is necessary for seeing.

In the patient's childhood home, not staying in the bandwidth created major trouble, as that was a situation with which the parents could not cope. In a different context, not staying in the childhood bandwidth may not even be noticed.

Gradually one may realize one was not taught a universal truth about living as a child. One was only taught how to make it easier for one's parents—and consequently for oneself. The price of this teaching had been that the child could not develop a real self and the experience necessary to use it.

It is not necessary to behave perfectly or do great things to be a real person and a worthwhile human being.

The good child must be welcomed into a context where the most important thing is being who he or she really is. Further, this is true regardless of whom he or she might upset or his or her success or failure in some specific situation.

Being one's true self is one's great gift to life. This is a person no one else can be. This is a person with thoughts and feelings unlike any other, one who has an important contribution to make simply by his or her presence. It is a person whose voice matters as it is unique. It is a person who is lovable.

Regardless of what the parents might think.

# REFERENCES

Benjamin, J.   The Bonds of Love: psychoanalysis, feminism, and the problem of domination. Pantheon, 1988.

Butler, J.  Gender Trouble: feminism and the subversion of identity.  Rutledge, 1999.

Chodorow, N.J.  Feminism and Psychoanalytic Theory.  Yale.  1989.

Diman, M. and Goldner, V. (Eds).  Gender in Psychoanalytic Space.  Other, 2002.

Flax, J. Thinking Fragments: psychoanalysis, feminism, and postmodernism in the contemporary west.  California, 1990.

Foucault, M.  The Order of Things: an archeology of the human sciences.  Random House, 1970.

Gabbard, G.O. Psychoanalytic Psychiatry in clinical practice.  APA, 2000.

Goldner, V.  "Toward a Critical Relationship Theory of Gender," in Diman, M. and Goldner, V.

(Eds), Gender in Psychoanalytic Space. Other, 2002.

Harlow, H.F. Learning to Love. Jones and Bartlett, 1971.

Miller, A. Drama of the Gifted Child.

Miller, A. Thou Shalt Not be Aware: society's betrayal of the child. Meridian, 1984.

Miller, A. For Your Own Good: hidden cruelty in child rearing and the roots of violence. FSG, 1983.

Mollon, P. The Fragile Self: the structure of narcissistic disturbance and it's therapy. Aronson, 1993.

Plath, S. "Daddy." In The Collected Poems. Harper, 2008.

Reedy, B. The Journey of the Heroic Parent: your child's struggle and the road home. Regan Arts, 2015.

Rilke, R.M. The Notebooks of Malte Laurids Brigge, trans. M.D.H. Norton. Norton. 1949.

Sartre, J.P. The Words [Les Mots]. Braziller, 1964.

Simmons, R.  Odd Girl Out: the hidden culture of aggression in girls.  Harcourt, 2002.

Siegel, D. J., and Hartzell, M.  Parenting from the Inside Out.  Tarcher/Penguin, 2003.

Winnicott, D.W.  Through Pediatrics to Psycho-Analysis.  Brunner/Mazel, 1992.

Wittgenstein, L.  Philosophical Investigations. Macmillan, 1953.

# ABOUT THE AUTHOR

J.D. Gill is a clinical psychologist at the University of Utah. She is an Adjunct Associate Professor of Psychology, a Clinical Professor of Counseling Psychology, and an Adjunct Associate Professor of Psychiatry in the University of Utah School of Medicine. Dr. Gill maintains a busy practice at the University of Utah.

Dr. Gill has degrees in English Literature, Philosophy, Psychology, and two post docs in psychoanalytic psychotherapy. She studied in the Writing Program at the University of Utah. She has been a practicing psychologist for over forty years and has presented over five hundred seminars, lectures, workshops, and papers. A world traveler, Dr. Gill has actively sought to experience multiple viewpoints and perspectives.

CPSIA information can be obtained
at www.ICGtesting.com
Printed in the USA
LVHW081606240920
666994LV00009B/3272

9 781514 874691